Flavors of the World – Belize

Over 25 Delicious Recipes You Can't Resist

BY: Nancy Silverman

COPYRIGHT NOTICES

My Heartfelt Thanks and A Special Reward for Your Purchase!

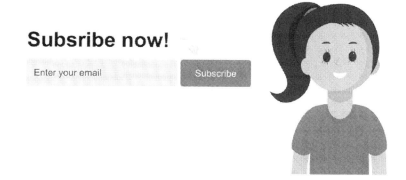

https://nancy.gr8.com

My heartfelt thanks at purchasing my book and I hope you enjoy it! As a special bonus, you will now be eligible to receive books absolutely free on a weekly basis! Get started by entering your email address in the box above to subscribe. A notification will be emailed to you of my free promotions, no purchase necessary! With little effort, you will be eligible for free and discounted books daily. In addition to this amazing gift, a reminder will be sent 1-2 days before the offer expires to remind you not to miss out. Enter now to start enjoying this special offer!

Table of Contents

25 Delicious Belizean Recipes

(1) Classic Brown Rice and Chicken

Last, we have this filling and simple Belizean dish that you can make. It is simple to prepare and one of the most classic Belizean recipes you will make. Regardless I know you are going to fall in love with it.

Serving Size: 6 Servings

Preparation Time: 2 Hours and 50 Minutes

Ingredient List:

- 2 teaspoons of Vinegar
- 2 teaspoons of Seasoning, All Purpose Variety
- 2 teaspoon of Jerk Seasoning, Medium in Spice
- 1, 8 Ounce Can of Chicken Soup, Condensed Variety
- Dash of Coconut, Powdered Variety
- 1, 8 Ounce Can of Peas and Carrots
- 1, 8 Ounce Can of Corn, Whole Kernel Variety
- 2 Cups of Chicken Breast, Cut into Small Sized Cubes
- 3 Cups of Brown Rice
- 8 Cups of Water, Warm

Instructions:

1. First cut up your chicken into small sized cubes. Then wash in some vinegar and set aside.

2. Clean and wash your rise thoroughly until the water runs clear.

3. Place your chicken into a large sized pot with your water to boil over high heat.

4. Once boiling add in your rice, chicken soup and jerk seasoning.

5. Reduce the heat to low and allow to cook for an additional 30 minutes, making sure to stir occasional until the liquid has completely evaporated.

6. Turn off the heat and add your peas and carrots on top of your rice.

7. Allow to sit for another 30 minutes before serving while still piping hot. Enjoy.

(2) Tomato and Pineapple Salsa

This delicious appetizer makes for a salsa that I know you are going to want to serve up as often as possible. It is simple to make and makes for a tasty treat that a whole group of people can easily enjoy.

Serving Size: 8 Servings

Preparation Time: 7 Minutes

Ingredients for Your Salsa:

- 2 Pounds of Tomatoes, Ripe and Finely Chopped
- 1 Onion, Medium in Size and Finely Chopped
- ¼ Cup of Cilantro, Fresh and Roughly Chopped
- 1 Pineapple, Small in Size, Ripe and Finely Chopped
- ¼ Cup of Basil, Fresh and Roughly Chopped

Ingredients for Your Vinegar Sauce:

- 2 Tablespoon of Vinegar, Pineapple and Basil Variety
- ½ to 1 Tablespoon of Brown Sugar, Light and Packed
- 2 Tablespoon of Pineapple, Juice Only and Fresh
- Dash of Garlic, Powdered Variety and for Taste
- Dash of Black Pepper, For Taste
- 1, 8 Ounce Can of Vienna's, Grace Variety and Thinly Sliced

IIIIIIIIIIIIIIIIIIIIIIIIIIIIIIIIIIIIIIIIIIIIIIIIIIIIIIIIIIII

Instructions:

1. First use a large sized bowl and mix all of your salsa ingredients together. Toss thoroughly until combined.

2. Season with a dash of salt and pepper.

3. Then use a medium sized separate bowl and mix together all of your ingredients for your sauce until evenly mixed and smooth in consistency.

4. Add this mixture into your salsa mixture and toss thoroughly until evenly combined.

5. Serve whenever you are ready.

(3) Filling Corn Casserole

Here is yet another casserole that I know you will want to make over and over again. It is filling and easy to make, making this the perfect dish to make if you want something easy to put together for your family.

Serving Size: 6 Servings

Preparation Time: 40 Minutes

Ingredient List:

- 1, 8 Ounce Can of Tuna, Light and Chunky Variety
- 1, 8 Ounce Can of Mixed Vegetables, Your Favorite Kind
- 3 Tablespoon of Mayonnaise, Your Favorite Kind
- 3 Tablespoon of Ketchup, Your Favorite Kind
- Dash of Hot Pepper Sauce
- 1 Onion, Small in Size and Finely Chopped
- 1 Tomato, Medium in Size and Finely Chopped
- 1 Bell Pepper, Small in Size, Red in Color and Finely Chopped
- Dash of Salt and Pepper, For Taste
- 6 Corn Tortillas, Fried

||||||||||||||||||||||||||||||||||||||||||||||||||||||||||

Instructions:

1. The first thing that you are going to want to do is drain your cans of tuna and mixed vegetables. Once drain add to a large sized bowl.

2. Add in your favorite mayonnaise, ketchup, onions, bell pepper and sliced tomato. Stir thoroughly to combine.

3. Season with a dash of salt and pepper.

4. Spoon over your fried tortillas and garnish with your hot sauce. Serve right away and enjoy.

(4) Belizean Hot Wings

If you are a huge fan of traditional hot wings, then this is one dish that you need to try for yourself. Keep in mind, these wings can be incredibly spicy so adjust the seasonings to fit your taste.

Serving Size: 2 Servings

Preparation Time: 15 Minutes

Ingredient List:

- 12 Pieces of Chicken, Wings and Bone in Variety
- 1 ½ Cups of Flour, All Purpose Variety
- ½ Tablespoon of Black Pepper, For Taste
- ½ Tablespoon of Chicken Consommé
- ½ Tablespoon of Seasoning, Malher Complete Variety
- 2 Cups of Oil, Coconut Variety
- 3 Tablespoon of Honey, Raw
- ½ Cup of Ketchup, Your Favorite Kind
- ½ Cup of Stout
- 1 Tablespoon of Pepper Sauce, Habanero Variety

III

Instructions:

1. First cut your chicken wings into two equal sized pieces. Then season with your seasonings.

2. Heat up your oil in a large sized skillet placed over high heat. While your oil is heating up place your flour into a zip lock bag and toss in your chicken wings. Shake vigorously to coat.

3. Once your oil is hot enough add in your chicken and cook for approximately 6 to 8 minutes or until thoroughly cooked through.

4. While your chicken is cooking mix your sauce together by mixing your ketchup and stout together. Add in your habanero sauce and stir thoroughly to combine.

5. Add this sauce to your wings and stir thoroughly to coat.

6. Serve whenever you are ready.

(5) Zesty Tuna Noodle Soup

This is another delicious dish that you can make if you are feeling a bit under the weather. Packed full of filling tuna, this is a dish that will have you feeling better in no time at all.

Serving Size: 4 Servings

Preparation Time: 2 Hours and 20 Minutes

Ingredient List:

- 4 Tablespoon of Chicken Consommé
- 1 Cup of Corn, Whole Kernel and Sweet Variety
- 1 Cup of Milk, Evaporated Variety
- 1, 8 Ounce Can of Tuna, In Water and Drained
- 1/8 teaspoon of Garlic, Powdered Variety
- 1, 8 Ounce Can of Cream of Mushroom Soup
- 1, 8 Ounce Can of Chicken Soup, Condensed Variety
- ¼ Cup of Water, Warm
- ¼ teaspoon of Basil, Dried Variety
- 2 Cups of Macaroni, Corkscrew Variety, Cooked and Drained

‖‖‖

Instructions:

1. The first thing that you will want to do is cook up your macaroni according to the directions on the package. Once cooked drain and set aside for later use.

2. Next add your tuna, chicken soup, corn, water, chicken consommé, fresh basil and powdered garlic into a large sized saucepan placed over high heat. Stir to combine and cook until boiling.

3. Once your mixture is boiling add in your corn and reduce the heat to low.

4. Continue to cook for an additional 10 minutes, making sure to stir occasionally.

5. Add in your milk, pasta and tuna. Continue to cook until completely heated through. Make sure to stir occasionally.

6. Remove from heat and serve with a garnish of fresh parsley. Enjoy.

(6) Corned Beef Style Hash Browns

While hash browns themselves can be delicious, when they are made out of Corned Beef. With these hash browns you can enjoy a treat that is more filling and packed full of a delicious taste that you won't be able to get enough of.

Serving Size: 10 Servings

Preparation Time: 10 Minutes

Ingredient List:

- 1 Pound of Potatoes
- ½ of an Onion, Small in Size and Finely Diced
- ½ Cup of Oil, Vegetable Variety
- ½ Cup of Cheese, Cheddar Variety and Freshly Grated
- 1 teaspoon of Garlic, Powdered Variety
- 1 teaspoon of Black Pepper, For Taste
- 1, 8 Ounce Can have Corned Beef, Your Favorite Kind

||||||||||||||||||||||||||||||||||||||||||||||||||||||||||||||||

Instructions:

1. The first thing that you want to do is peel and wash your potatoes. Grate them finely and then wash again. Add to a large sized bowl.

2. Add in your remaining ingredients and stir to combine.

3. Next heat up some oil in a large sized skillet placed over high heat.

4. Once your oil is hot enough add in a small scoop of your corn beef mixture and make sure to flatten.

5. Fry on both sides until brown in color.

6. Once brown place onto a plate lined with paper towels to drain and serve while still piping hot. Enjoy.

(7) Jalapeno Style Potato Casserole

If you are looking for a dish that will satisfy and feed your entire family, then this is the perfect dish for you to make. Easy to prepare and packed full of just the right amount of spice, I can guarantee your family will be begging for more of this recipe.

Serving Size: 12 Servings

Preparation Time: 1 Hour and 15 Minutes

Ingredient List:

- 1, 16 Ounce Can of Milk, Evaporated Variety
- ½ Tablespoon of Garlic, Powdered Variety
- 1, 5 Ounce Can of Jalapenos, Freshly Sliced
- ¼ teaspoon of Seasoning, All Purpose Variety
- Dash of Hot Sauce, Your Favorite Kind
- 3 Pounds of Potatoes, Medium in Size and Finely Diced
- 1 Pound of Cheese, Freshly Grated
- 1 Onion, Large in Size and Finely Diced
- 1 Sweet Pepper, Medium in Size and Finely Diced
- 2 Ounces of Margarine, Soft
- 2 ½ Cups of Water, Warm
- ¼ Cup of Flour, All Purpose Variety

IIIIIIIIIIIIIIIIIIIIIIIIIIIIIIIIIIIIIIIIIIIIIIIIIIIIIIIIIIIIIIIII

Instructions:

1. First mince your sweet peppers and onions finely. Set aside for later use.

2. Then place your margarine into a large sized skillet placed over medium heat. Once your butter is melted add in your flour and stir thoroughly to combine. Cook for at least 1 minutes.

3. Add in your milk and continue to cook until thick in consistency.

4. Next peel your potatoes and slice them thinly. Season with your powdered garlic and all-purpose seasoning.

5. Generously grease a large sized baking dish and pour in at least ½ cup of water into it. Add in your potato slices and cover. Place into your oven to bake at 350 degrees for the next 15 minutes.

6. After this time remove from oven and add in your onions, sweet pepper and hot sauce. Stir thoroughly to combine.

7. Top off with your cheese and milk mixture. Toss to combine.

8. Place back into your oven to bake for another 20 minutes.

9. Remove from your oven and serve while still piping hot. Enjoy.

(8) Classic Tuna Ceviche

This is as traditional as it gets when it comes to Belizean recipes. This delicious dish is incredibly delicious and is perfect for those who are huge fans of seafood.

Serving Size: 8 Servings

Preparation Time: 15 Minutes

Ingredient List:

- 1, 4 Ounce Can of Tuna, in Water and Drained
- 1 Sweet Pepper, Medium in Size and Finely Diced
- 2 Tomatoes, Medium in Size and Finely Diced
- 1 Onion, Medium in Size and Finely Diced
- 1 Carrot, Fresh, Small in Size and Finely Diced
- 6 Limes, Fresh and Juice Only
- 4 Sprigs of Cilantro, Fresh and Roughly Chopped
- ½ teaspoon of Black Pepper, For Taste
- Dash of Salt, For Taste
- 1 teaspoon of Garlic, Powdered Variety
- 1 Tablespoon of Pepper Sauce, Habanero Variety
- Some Corn Tortilla Chips, For Serving

‖‖‖

Instructions:

1. Use a large sized bowl and combine all of your ingredients together except for your tortilla chips. Toss thoroughly to combine.

2. Pour your mixture into a small sized bowl and place onto a plate.

3. Add your tortilla chips around your main salsa dish and serve whenever you are ready.

(9) Christmas Style Chocolate Cake

This is a decadent dessert dish that you are going to want to prepare during the Christmas holiday. Smothered in a decadent cocoa frosting, this cake is a chocoholics dream.

Serving Size: 6 Servings

Preparation Time: 1 Hour and 25 Minutes

Ingredient List:

- 1, 8 Ounce Can of Milk, Evaporated Variety
- 4 Tablespoon of Cocoa, Heaping
- 4 Tablespoon of Instant Chocolate, Heaping
- 2 Cups of Sugar, Granulated Variety
- ¾ Cup of Butter, Soft
- 3 Eggs, Large in Size and Beaten
- 1 ½ teaspoon of Vanilla, Pure
- 2 Cups of Flour, All Purpose Variety
- Dash of Salt, For Taste
- Dash of Baker's Style Baking Soda

Ingredients for Your Cocoa Frosting:

- 3 Tablespoon of Butter, Soft
- ¼ Cup of Cocoa
- 2 Tablespoon of Milk, Evaporated Variety
- 1 1/3 Cup of Sugar, Powdered Variety
- ½ teaspoon of Vanilla, Pure
- 1 Cup of Nuts, Optional and Your Favorite Kind

IIIIIIIIIIIIIIIIIIIIIIIIIIIIIIIIIIIIIIIIIIIIIIIIIIIIIIIIIIIII

Instructions:

1. The first thing that you will want to do is whip together your butter and sugar in a medium sized bowl until evenly mixed.

2. Add in your eggs again and stir again to combine.

3. Add in your flour, cocoa, instant chocolate, dash of salt, baker's style baking soda, evaporated milk and vanilla. Mix well to combine.

4. Pour this mixture into a generously greased baking dish.

5. Place into your oven to bake at 350 degrees for the next 20 to 25 minutes.

6. While your cake is baking make your frosting. To do this use a small sized bowl and mix together all of your frosting ingredients until smooth in consistency.

7. Remove your cake from your oven and allow to cool completely before spreading your frosting over the top.

8. Garnish with nuts and serve whenever you are ready.

(10) Honey Glazed Chicken Wings

If you wish to enjoy chicken wings but don't want to handle the spice often associated with them, then this is the perfect dish for you. Smothered in a honey glaze this is a perfect dish to make to help satisfy your strongest sweet tooth.

Serving Size: 6 Servings

Preparation Time: 1 Hour and 15 Minutes

Ingredient List:

- ½ Cup of Flour, All Purpose Variety
- 1 teaspoon of Salt, For Taste
- ½ teaspoon of Cayenne Pepper, For Taste
- 3 Pounds of Chicken Wings, Bone in Variety
- ½ Cup of Butter, Fully Melted
- ½ Cup of Brown Sugar, Light and Packed
- ¼ Cup of Honey, Raw
- ¼ Cup of Lemon, Juice Only and Fresh
- 1 Tablespoon of Soy Sauce, Your Favorite Kind
- 1 ½ teaspoon of Curry, Powdered Variety

||||||||||||||||||||||||||||||||||||||||||||||||||||||||||||

Instructions:

1. Use a large sized bowl and add in your flour, salt and cayenne pepper. Stir thoroughly to combine.

2. Once mixed add in your chicken wings and dredge on all sides to coat.

3. Then add in your butter into a large sized baking dish.

4. Place your chicken into this dish and place into your oven to bake at 350 degrees for the next 30 minutes.

5. While your chicken is baking mix together your brown sugar, fresh lemon juice, honey, favorite soy sauce, powdered curry and remaining butter. Stir thoroughly to combine.

6. Remove your chicken from your oven and pour your sauce over the top.

7. Place back into your oven to bake for an additional 45 minutes or until tender to the touch.

8. Remove and allow to cool slightly before serving.

(11) Fiesta Style Taco Salad

Here is yet another Mexican Inspired Belizean dish that I know you are going to fall in love with. This is a great tasting salad dish to make for those looking for something on the healthier side as well as something that will satisfy their taste buds.

Serving Size: 6 Servings

Preparation Time: 3 Hours

Ingredient List:

- 1, 14 Ounce Can of Corned Beef, Your Favorite Kind
- 1 Tablespoon of Oil, Coconut Variety
- 1, 14 Ounce Can of Kidney Beans, Red in Color
- 1 Tablespoon of Fish Sauce
- 2 Tablespoon of Chili, Powdered Variety
- ½, 8 Ounce Can of Tomato Soup, Your Favorite Kind
- 8 Cups of Lettuce, Green in Color and Freshly Shredded
- 2 Cups of Tortilla Chips, Your Favorite Kind
- 1 Container of Sour Cream, Small in Size
- 1 Tomato, Large in Size and Finely Chopped
- 2 Ounces of Green Onion, Thinly Sliced
- 2 Cups of Cheddar Cheese, Freshly Shredded
- 1/2, 8 Ounce Can of Black Olives, Pitted and Thinly Sliced

||||||||||||||||||||||||||||||||||||||||||||||||||||||||||||||

Instructions:

1. Use a medium sized skillet set over medium to high heat and cook your corned beef, oil fish sauce and powdered chili. Cook until brown in color.

2. Add in your kidney beans and tomato soup.

3. Reduce the heat to low and cook until thick in consistency.

4. Arrange your chips neatly on a serving platter and place your lettuce over the top.

5. Spoon your meat and bean mixture over your lettuce.

6. Top off with your olive, tomatoes, sour cream, green onions and cheddar cheese. Serve right away and enjoy.

(12) Creamy Belizean Cheese Dip

Here is yet another dip recipe that I know you won't be able to get enough of. For the tastiest results I highly recommend serving it with crackers or your favorite tortilla chips. Either way I know you are going to love it.

Serving Size: 5 Servings

Preparation Time: 25 Minutes

Ingredient List:

- 1 Pound of Cheese, Processed and Your Favorite Kind
- 1, 8 Ounce Can of Milk, Fully Evaporated
- 1, 5 Ounce of Salsa, Your Favorite Kind
- Dash of Pepper, For Taste

||||||||||||||||||||||||||||||||||||||||||||||||||||||||||||||||||||||||

Instructions:

1. Place all of your ingredients into a food processor.

2. Blend on the highest setting thoroughly until smooth in consistency.

3. Pour into a serving dish and serve with your favorite tortilla chips. Enjoy.

(13) Tasty Shrimp and Noodle Chowder

This is a delicious soup recipe that you can make if you are looking for a healthier and more filling recipe to make. It is certainly a dish that you can make to keep you feeling warm during the cold winter months.

Serving Size: 4 Servings

Preparation Time: 15 Minutes

Ingredient List:

- ½ Pound of Shrimp, Fresh, Shelled and Deveined
- 1 Onion, Large in Size and Finely Chopped
- 1, 4 Ounce Can of Whole Kernel Corn
- 1, 8 Ounce Can of Milk, Evaporated Variety
- 1, 8 Ounce Can of Cream of Mushroom Soup
- 3 Cups of Chicken Noodle Soup, Your Favorite Kind
- 2 Tablespoon of Garlic, Powdered Variety
- ½ Cup of Water, Warm

||||||||||||||||||||||||||||||||||||||||||||||||||||||||||

Instructions:

1. The first thing that you will want to do is cook up your noodle soup according to the directions on the package. Once cooked set aside for later use.

2. Then use a medium sized saucepan and mix together your cream of mushroom soup, powdered garlic and cooked noodle soup. Stir thoroughly to combine.

3. Cover and heat over high heat for the next 2 to 3 minutes.

4. Add in your corn and reduce the heat to low.

5. Add in your shrimp, onion and milk.

6. Continue to cook for another 5 minutes or until your shrimp turns pink in color.

7. Remove from heat and serve while still piping hot.

(14) Fiesta Style Bean Soup

If you are looking for something on the spicier side and that is still incredibly filling, then this is the perfect dish for you to make. Serve this dish with your favorite tortilla chips to make it truly delicious.

Serving Size: 6 Servings

Preparation Time: 25 Minutes

Ingredient List:

- 1 Pound of Kidney Beans, Red in Color
- 1 Pound of Pinto Beans, Stewed Variety
- 1 Onion, Medium in Size and Finely Diced
- 1 Sweet Pepper, Medium in Size and Finely Diced
- 1, 8 Ounce Can of Corn, Whole Kernel Variety
- 1, 8 Ounce Can of Mushrooms, Thinly Sliced
- 3 Tablespoon of Consome, Malher Variety
- ½ Tablespoon of Milk, Coconut Variety and Powdered Variety
- 2 Tablespoon of Cumin, Ground Variety
- 2 Tablespoon of Chili, Powdered Variety
- ½ Tablespoon of Seasonings, Complete Variety
- 2 Tablespoon of Black Pepper, For Taste
- Dash of Bay Leaves, Fresh
- 2 Tablespoon of Oil, Vegetable Variety

||||||||||||||||||||||||||||||||||||||||||||||||||||||||

Instructions:

1. Using a large sized pot heat up your oil over medium heat. Once the oil is hot enough add in your onions and sweet peppers. Cook until your onions are translucent.

2. Add in your corn and mushrooms and continue to cook for an additional 3 minutes.

3. After this time add in your kidney and pinto beans.

4. Season with some black pepper and seasoning. Add in your powdered chili, cumin fresh bay leaves and consommé.

5. Add in your powdered milk and allow to cook for an additional 10 to 15 minutes before remove from heat.

6. Allow to cool slightly before serving.

(15) Delicious Vienna Sausage Pancakes

This is a great tasting breakfast recipe that I know you won't be able to get enough of. Absolutely filling, this is a delicious early morning treat to enjoy regardless of the day.

Serving Size: 2 Servings

Preparation Time: 40 Minutes

Ingredient List:

- 1 Egg, Whole and Beaten
- 1 Cup of Flour, All Purpose Variety
- ¾ Cup of Milk, Evaporated Variety
- 1 Tablespoon of Sugar, White
- 2 ½ Tablespoon of Oil, Vegetable Variety
- 1 Tablespoon of Baker's Style Baking Powder
- ½ teaspoon of Salt, For Taste
- ¼ Cup of Cheese, Cheddar Variety and Freshly Grated
- ¼ Cup of Sweet Peppers, Red in Color and Finely Chopped
- 1, 4 Ounce Can of Vienna Sausages, Jalapeno Variety

IIIIIIIIIIIIIIIIIIIIIIIIIIIIIIIIIIIIIIIIIIIIIIIIIIIIIIIIIIIIIII

Instructions:

1. Using a large sized bowl and mix together all of your ingredients except for your sausages, cheese and sweet peppers until smooth in consistency.

2. Then heat up some oil in a large sized skillet over medium heat.

3. Once your oil is hot enough add in a spoonful of your batter and allow to cook for the next five minutes.

4. After this time add in your sausages and continue to cook until brown in color. Flip and continue to cook until brown on this side as well.

5. Remove from heat and top off with your cheddar cheese and sweet peppers. Repeat until all of your batter has been used. Serve whenever you are ready.

(16) Coconut Style Chicken Soup

Here is a chicken soup recipe that you can make if you are feeling under the weather. It is so delicious it will leave you feeling better in no time.

Serving Size: 4 Servings

Preparation Time: 40 Minutes

Ingredient List:

- 1, 2 Inch Piece of Ginger, Peeled and Sliced Thinly
- 2 Cups of Milk, Coconut Variety
- 1 Cup of Chicken Stock, Homemade Variety
- 3 Chicken Breast Fillets, Cut into Thin Strips
- 1 to 2 teaspoon of Chilies, Red in Color and Finely Chopped
- 2 Tablespoon of Fish Sauce
- 1 teaspoon of Brown Sugar, Light and Packed
- ¼ Cup of Cilantro, Fresh and Roughly Chopped

||||||||||||||||||||||||||||||||||||||||||||||||||||||||||||

Instructions:

1. First combine your ginger, chicken stock and milk in a medium sized saucepan. Set over medium heat and bring your mixture to a boil.

2. Once your mixture is boiling reduce the heat to low and allow to simmer for the next 10 minutes, making sure to stir occasionally.

3. Add your chicken and chilies to your skillet and allow to simmer for the next 8 minutes.

4. Add in your fish sauce and brown sugar. Toss thoroughly to coat.

5. Add in your cilantro and remove from heat.

6. Serve with a garnish of cilantro and enjoy while piping hot.

(17) Simple French Toast

Here is yet another great tasting breakfast dish that I know you won't be able to get enough of. It is incredibly easy to make and will surely satisfy even the pickiest of eaters.

Serving Size: 5 Servings

Preparation Time: 40 Minutes

Ingredient List:

- 4 Eggs, Large in Size and Beaten Lightly
- ¾ Cup of Milk, Evaporated Variety
- 3 Tablespoon of Brown Sugar, Light and Packed
- 1 teaspoon of Nutmeg, Ground Variety
- 12 Slices of Bread, White in Color
- 1 Tablespoon of Cinnamon, Ground Variety

||||||||||||||||||||||||||||||||||||||||||||||||||||||||||||||||

Instructions:

1. Use a large sized mixing bowl and beat together your eggs until evenly mixed and thoroughly beaten.

2. Add in your milk, packed brown sugar and nutmeg. Beat again until combined.

3. Add in your bread slices and soak until your bread has been fully saturated.

4. While your bread is soaking heat up a large sized skillet with some oil placed over medium heat.

5. Once the oil is hot enough add in your bread and cook on both sides until brown in color.

6. Remove and serve with a dash of cinnamon.

(18) Light Avocado Salad

Are you a huge fan of salad? If so I know this is one salad recipe you are going to want to make over and over again. Feel free to add whatever veggies you wish to this salad to truly make it your own.

Serving Size: 4 Servings

Preparation Time: 10 Minutes

Ingredient List:

- 2 Avocados, Fresh and Finely Diced
- 4 Cups of Lettuce, Fresh and Shredded
- 2 Tomatoes, Medium in Size and Thinly Sliced
- 1 Onion, Small in Size and Finely Diced
- 1, 8 Ounce Can of Carrots and Peas
- 1, 8 Ounce Can of Corn, Whole Kernel Variety
- 1 Sweet Pepper, Medium in Size and Finely Diced
- 1 Cucumber, Large in Size and Thinly Sliced
- 2 teaspoon of Oregano, Fresh
- ¼ teaspoon of Garlic, Powdered Variety
- ¼ teaspoon of Black Pepper, For Taste
- 6 teaspoon of Vinegar, White in Color
- 2 teaspoon of Sugar, White in Color

||||||||||||||||||||||||||||||||||||||||||||||||||||||||||||

Instructions:

1. The first thing that you will want to do is rinse all of your vegetables and place into a large sized bowl.

2. Using a separate large sized bowl mix together your vinegar, oil, powdered garlic and oregano. Whisk thoroughly until smooth in consistency.

3. Drain your peas and carrots and mix together with your corn, sweet peppers and finely diced avocado.

4. Pour your dressing over your vegetables and toss thoroughly to mix.

5. Place onto a large sized serving dish and spoon your veggie mixture over the top.

6. Layer your tomato and cucumber over the top.

7. Garnish with some fresh cilantro and serve whenever you are ready.

(19) Simple Coconut Bread

If you have those in your household who are bread eaters and want to satisfy their taste buds, then this is the perfect dish for you to make. This makes a lot of bread so don't hesitate to make as much of it as you want.

Serving Size: 4 Servings

Preparation Time: 1 Hour and 5 Minutes

Ingredient List:

- 2 Cups of Flour, All Purpose Variety
- 1 Tablespoon of Baker's Style Baking Powder
- 1/8 teaspoon of Salt, For Taste
- ½ Cup of Sugar, White
- 1 Egg, Large in Size and Beaten Lightly
- ¼ Cup of Milk, Coconut Variety
- 6 Tablespoon of Margarine, Fully Melted
- ½ teaspoon of Vanilla, Pure
- 6 Tablespoon of Raisins, Floured Variety and Your Favorite Kind
- ½ of a Coconut, Small in Size, Peeled and Freshly Grated

||||||||||||||||||||||||||||||||||||||||||||||||||||||||

Instructions:

1. First preheat your oven to 350 degrees.

2. While your oven is heating up stir your flour, baker's style baking powder, dash of salt and sugar together in a large sized bowl until evenly mixed.

3. Use another bowl and mix together your eggs and coconut milk until evenly mixed. Add in your vanilla, raisins, coconut, and soft margarine. Stir again.

4. Add this mixture into your dry ingredients and stir thoroughly until a dough begins to form.

5. Knead your dough on a lightly floured surface until smooth in texture.

6. Place into a generously greased loaf pan.

7. Place into your oven to bake for the next 45 minutes or until thoroughly baked through and golden in color.

8. Remove and allow to cool slightly before serving. Enjoy.

(20)   Vegetarian Style Sweet Corn Soup

Here is a sweet tasting soup recipe that you can make for your vegetarian or vegan friends and family. Easy to make and surprisingly filling, this is a great lunch dish that I know you are going to fall in love with.

Serving Size: 10 Servings

Preparation Time: 17 Minutes

Ingredient List:

- 1, 8 Ounce Can of Corn, Cream Style
- ½ Cup of Corn, Whole Kernel Variety
- 1, 8 Ounce Can of Mixed Vegetables, Your Favorite Kind
- 5 Cups of Water, Warm
- 3 Tablespoon of Milk, Evaporated Variety
- 2 ½ Tablespoon of Corn Starch
- ¾ Tablespoon of Sugar, White
- Dash of Salt, For Taste
- 2 Tablespoon of Oil, Coconut Variety
- 1 Tablespoon of Soy Sauce, Your Favorite Kind

|||||||||||||||||||||||||||||||||||||||||||||||||||||||||||||

Instructions:

1. Using a large sized pot add in your sweet corn and water. Set over medium heat.

2. Add in your mixed veggies and cook for at least 5 minutes before adding in your corn and milk. Stir to combine.

3. Continue to cook for another 2 minutes.

4. Using a medium sized bowl add in your cornstarch with at least 4 spoonfuls of water. Mix well until your cornstarch dissolves. Set aside for later use.

5. Add your sugar into your simmer soup and continue to cook for another 3 to 4 minutes before adding in your soy sauce.

6. Season with a dash of salt.

7. Add your cornstarch mixture into your soup and stir thoroughly until thick in consistency.

8. Add in your oil and continue to cook for another 5 minutes before removing from heat. Serve while still piping hot and enjoy.

(21) Classic Garifuna Porridge

If you are looking for something on the lighter side to enjoy but that is still incredibly easy to make, then this is the perfect dish for you to make. It is so delicious even the smallest of children are going to fall in love with this recipe.

Serving Size: 6 Servings

Preparation Time: 10 Minutes

Ingredient List:

- ½ Cup of Gungude, Powdered Variety
- 3 Cups of Water, Warm
- 1/2 of an 8 Ounce Can of Milk, Condensed Variety
- ½ of an 8 Ounce Can of Milk, Powdered Variety
- 1 Tablespoon of Milk, Coconut Variety and Powdered Variety
- Dash of Salt, For Taste
- 2 teaspoons of Vanilla, Pure
- 2 teaspoons of Nutmeg

||||||||||||||||||||||||||||||||||||||||||||||||||||||||||||||||

Instructions:

1. Using a large sized deep pot, add in your water and bring to a boil over medium heat.

2. Pour in at least 1 cup of water into a small sized bowl and add in your gungude. Stir thoroughly to combine and pour back into your boiling water.

3. Add in your condensed and powdered milk.

4. Continue to stir for another 5 to 10 minutes or until thick in consistency. Season with a dash of salt.

5. Remove from heat and garnish with your vanilla and nutmeg.

(22)   Traditional Nahil Mayab Salad

Here is a healthy summer time salad if you are looking for something on the lighter side. It is easy to put together and makes for a great tasting lunch dish to enjoy free of any guilt.

Serving Size: 2 Servings

Preparation Time: 2 Hours and 5 Minutes

Ingredient List:

- 1 Head of Lettuce, Romaine Variety
- 1 Avocado, Large in Size, Ripe Peeled and Sliced Thinly
- 1 Mango, Large in Size, Seeded, Peeled and Sliced Thinly
- 1 Tomato, Medium in Size and Cut into Wedges

IIIIIIIIIIIIIIIIIIIIIIIIIIIIIIIIIIIIIIIIIIIIIIIIIIIIIIIIIIIIIIII

Instructions:

1. Use a large sized serving plate and arrange your lettuce, mango and avocado.

2. Arrange your tomatoes around your lettuce and mango mixture.

3. Top off with your corn and serve right away.

(23)   Sweet Cinnamon Rolls

Want something more on the sweet side to enjoy in the morning? Then this is the perfect dish for you to make. These classic cinnamon rolls are incredibly easy to make and are some of the most delicious cinnamon rolls that you will ever enjoy.

Serving Size: 3 Servings

Preparation Time: 2 Hours and 15 Minutes

Ingredient List:

- 2 Cups of Flour, All Purpose Variety
- 4 teaspoons of Baker's Style Baking Powder
- ½ teaspoon of Salt, For Taste
- ½ teaspoon of Sugar, White in Color
- ¼ Cup of Shortening, Soft
- ¾ Cup of Milk, Evaporated Variety

Ingredients for Your Glaze:

- 3 Tablespoon of Cinnamon, Ground Variety
- ¼ Cup of Sugar, White

||||||||||||||||||||||||||||||||||||||||||||||||||||||||||||

Instructions:

1. The first thing that you will want to do is preheat your oven to 400 degrees.

2. While your oven is heating up use a large sized bowl and mix together your flour, baker's style baking powder and salt until evenly mixed.

3. Then add in your shortening and milk and mix again until your dough is firm to the touch.

4. Flatten out your dough into a rectangle that is at least ¼ inch in thickness.

5. Sprinkle the top of your dough with some sugar and powdered cinnamon.

6. Roll your dough jelly roll style and slice into even sized pieces.

7. Place your slices onto a generously greased baking sheet and place into your oven to bake at 400 degrees for the next 15 to 20 minutes.

8. While your rolls are baking making your glaze. To do this mix your ingredients for your glaze in a small sized bowl until smooth in consistency.

9. Remove your rolls from your oven and place on a wire rack to cool. Drizzle your glaze over the top while still hot and enjoy while still warm.

(24)   Curried and Coconut Seafood Soup

Here is a delicious seafood soup recipe that you can make if you are a huge fan of seafood. Feel free to add in your favorite kind of seafood to make this dish truly unique and delicious.

Serving Size: 8 Servings

Preparation Time: 22 Minutes

Ingredient List:

- 2 Snappers, Whole and Fresh
- 8 Ounces of Shrimp, Peeled and Deveined
- 4 Sea Crabs, Fresh
- 2 Tablespoon of Oil, Coconut Variety
- 1 Onion, Small in Size and Thinly Sliced
- 2 Cloves of Garlic, Finely Diced
- 4 Tablespoon of Curry, Powdered Variety
- 3 Tablespoon of Tomato Paste
- 2, 4 Ounce Cans of Milk, Coconut Variety
- 2 Tablespoon of Chicken Consome
- 1 Ounce of Ginger, Fresh and Grated
- Dash of Black Pepper, For Taste
- Dash of Basil, Fresh and Roughly Chopped
- Dash of Cilantro, Fresh and Roughly Chopped

|||||||||||||||||||||||||||||||||||||||||||||||||||||||||||||||||||

Instructions:

1. First use a large sized saucepot and heat up your oil over medium heat. Once the oil is hot enough add in your onions, garlic and ginger. Cook for at least 3 to 4 minutes or until your onions are translucent.

2. Use a separate bowl add in your seasoning. Set aside.

3. Add your snapper, crab and shrimp to your pot and cook until thoroughly brown on all sides.

4. Add in your powdered curry and tomato paste. Stir again to combine.

5. Then add in your milk and allow your mixture to simmer for the next 8 minutes.

6. Season with your seasoning and pepper.

7. Reduce the heat to low and add in your fresh cilantro and basil.

8. Allow to simmer for another 2 minutes before removing from heat. Serve while still piping hot and enjoy.

(25)   Summer Time Breakfast

Just as the name implies this is a great tasting dish to make during the summer months. For the tastiest results I highly recommend serving this dish with a slice of fresh avocado.

Serving Size: 4 Servings

Preparation Time: 10 Minutes

Ingredient List:

- 1, 8 Ounce Can of Corned Beef
- ½ of an Onion, Small in Size and Finely Diced
- ½ of a Sweet Pepper, Small in Size and Finely Diced
- 2 Tablespoon of Oil, Vegetable Variety
- 2 teaspoons of Consome, Malher Variety
- 1 Avocado, Fresh and Ripe
- 6 Tablespoon of Cream, Salad Variety
- 3 Tablespoon of Mustard
- 1 Tablespoon of Seasonings, Complete Variety
- A Few Lettuce Leaves, Fresh
- 1 Tomato, Small in Size and Thinly Sliced

||||||||||||||||||||||||||||||||||||||||||||||||||||||||||||||

Instructions:

1. The first thing that you will want to do is add your malher to your eggs.

2. Then heat up your oil in a large sized skillet placed over medium heat. Once the oil is hot enough add in your sweet peppers and onions. Cook for at least one to 3 minutes or until your onions are tender to the touch.

3. Next add in your corned beef and stir thoroughly to combine. Cook for another 5 minutes before removing from heat and set aside.

4. Mash your avocado with your seasoning until evenly mixed together.

5. Use a separate bowl and mix your salad cream and mustard together until smooth in consistency.

6. Spread your mustard mixture onto a slice of toasted bread. Add your mashed avocado and lettuce.

7. Top off with your corned beef mixture and sliced tomatoes. Top off with another slice of bread and serve right away.

About the Author

Nancy Silverman is an accomplished chef and cookbook author from Essex, Vermont. She attended Essex High School where she graduated with honors then moved on to University of Vermont where she received a degree in Nutrition and Food Sciences. She later attended New England Culinary Institute located close to her home town of Essex, in Montpelier, Vermont.

Nancy met her husband at school in Vermont when the two were set up on a date by a mutual friend. Both shared a love of the culinary arts and it was love at first sight! Nancy and Dennis have been married for 16 years and live on a beautiful property close to Nancy's childhood home in Essex. They have 3 children and 2 golden retrievers named Lucy and Ricky.

Nancy loves growing her own vegetables and herbs in the garden she has cultivated and cared for in the family's spacious backyard. Her greatest joy is cooking in her modern kitchen with her family and creating inspiring and delicious meals. She often says that she has perfected her signature dishes based on her family's critique of each and every one.

Nancy has her own catering company and has also been fortunate enough to be head chef at some of Vermont's most exclusive restaurants. She aspires to open her own restaurant, but for now she is content working from home and building her catering empire with the help of her children. When a friend suggested she share some of her outstanding signature dishes, she decided to add cookbook author to her repertoire of personal achievements. Being a technological savvy woman, she felt the e-book realm would be a better fit and soon she had her first cookbook available online. As of today, Nancy has sold over 1,000 e-books and has shared her culinary experiences and brilliant recipes with people from all over the world! She plans on expanding into self-help books and dietary cookbooks, so stayed tuned!

Author's Afterthoughts

Thank you for making the decision to invest in one of my cookbooks! I cherish all my readers and hope you find joy in preparing these meals as I have.

There are so many books available and I am truly grateful that you decided to buy this one and follow it from beginning to end.

I love hearing from my readers on what they thought of this book and any value they received from reading it. As a personal favor, I would appreciate any feedback you can give in the form of a review on Amazon and please be honest! This kind of support will help others make an informed choice on and will help me tremendously in producing the best quality books possible.

My most heartfelt thanks,

Nancy Silverman

If you're interested in more of my books, be sure to follow my author page on Amazon (can be found on the link Bellow) or scan the QR-Code.

https://www.amazon.com/author/nancy-silverman

Printed in Great Britain
by Amazon